CROWNHILL

REFLECTIONS

Arthur L. Clamp

Donkey Rowe, a beloved local character, is seen here with his
donkeys hauling wood up from Tamerton Foliot.

This version of the book is virtually as originally published.
There are now additional pages at the back providing information about the author.

The republishing project is being managed by Arthur's grandson, Steven Gibson. We aim to find all the research that he was involved in publishing, preserving it for the next generation as part of 'The Clamp Collection'.

THIS illustrated booklet can be divided into two sections, recollections of Crownhill mainly between the two world wars by Mr. S. J. Russell who spent his boyhood days here and the miscellaneous arrangements of photographs showing various aspects of the locality and people who have contributed in one way or another to the life of the village. There are many other photographs available and many further descriptions could be written which would extend the coverage of this title but these must be left to another day.

Crownhill or Knackersnowle, to give the former name of the area, was born between two parishes, St. Budeaux and Eggbuckland, the Tavistock main road forming the boundary at least for part of the way through the village and at the corner of Peverell parish. The name Crownhill was adopted sometime during the 1880s although the original settlement had been in being for probably a hundred years or more. The reason for a community growing here at all was primarily one of convenience on a road system which had been developed through the Turnpike Trusts linking Plymouth to Tavistock. Eggbuckland village was bypassed and St. Budeaux itself was too far to the west although both parishes did have control over the area right up until recent times. Crownhill was incorporated into the city area in 1939 and from that date it became the responsibility of Plymouth.

The development of the area first occurred at the top of Budshead Road where the former Holy Trinity chapel of Ease stands (built in 1843) then from the main road crossroads created when the Tavistock Road was turnpiked. Private houses, businesses and, of course, the numerous military accommodation blocks covered once well known fields and by the 1960s made the area almost indistinguishable from the rest of the northern part of Plymouth which had also been developed in various directions. Crownhill was virtually bisected when the very large flyover and feeder roads were built in the late 1960s causing yet another significant change in the shape of the village and the manner in which people could walk around the roads and terraces which once made up part of the heart of the locality. A good appreciation of these later changes can be obtained by looking at the photograph on the back cover of this book (1927) and the 1919 map. A comparison between those years and today should sharpen one's awareness of how quickly a familiar place can change.

In spite of these changes Crownhill does have its own character and many families who have made it their homestead for years will quickly rebuff any undue comment or comparison made with much older communities or places which claim a long standing parish church, castle or other prominent feature.

Perhaps Crownhill's claim can be for its now one hundred years and more association with the military authorities first through the construction of the large Crownhill Fort in the 1860s then the Barracks in the 1890s and now the extensive Seaton Barracks. This presence also determined to some extent the development of shops, the provision of community activities and the inhabitants who settled here. A much older role was in its farming activities, large country houses, extensive woodlands and the wide range of pursuits linked to these as referred to by S. J. Russell. This area was obviously a very desirable country locality years ago when leadership came from well established families living as lords of the manor. Their influence in the annual calendar of local events frequently makes itself felt in early accounts of life at Crownhill.

An interesting range of activities can be gleaned from trade directories and maps showing the site of the blacksmiths' shops, the toll gate, the old coach works, abattoir, old village halls, forage merchants, the leat and waterworks, the very early mills, farms and horticultural holdings, old post office, saddlers, tailors, schools, dairymen, butchers, bakers and a host of other minor, yet important, forms of employment.

Church and chapels have been and still are part of the pattern of local living. A Methodist Chapel was registered here as early as 1812, then came the Chapel of Ease linked with St. Budeaux Church, the Garrison Church played its role and now modern places of worship serve the community. Public inns, horse-drawn coaches through to Tavistock, and then the first cars impressed themselves in the minds of people when recalling the times of yesterday.

The changes and developments over the last few decades have produced a Crownhill of quite a different complexion with good access into the city, residential properties of a high standard and an ever increasing number of people coming into the area and setting up home here. The village is no longer separate from Plymouth or indeed on its edge but now part of a large sweep of the city reaching out as far as Roborough.

The preparation of this title was not the work of just one person but of many who made suggestions, lent photographs, stimulated memories and gave of their time. It was through the suggestion and later the notes of S. J. Russell, now living in Wales, that steps were first made towards its compilation. My thanks must first go to him then to Jon Massey, for his local work, and to many others including Jim Sykes, Bill Evans, J. R. Riley, Mrs. A. E. Lane, Mrs. W. Charlton, Mrs. MacGill, Mr. Congdon, Miss G. Denley, Mrs. A Blake and Mr. Rendle. I hope this title will at least form a permanent record of part of the life-style of yesterday's Crownhill and be a reminder of the not too distant days when it was quite a separate village surrounded by fields on the edge of Plymouth.

REMINISCENCES OF THE VILLAGE

Some years ago I stood at Raymond's corner in Crownhill, Plymouth, and was looking westwards across the teeming roads of the new flyover when I caught sight of a small, newly–painted corrugated building which was then doing service as a kindergarden. It's services no longer required it has now gone, but that innocuous little building – a shed almost – brought back more than a few memories of a Crownhill of long ago; and in particular a memory of a certain evening, when as a boy of around ten years I provided (probably somewhat sketchy) a sort of "running commentary" to a magic lantern show held before an enthusiastic audience of a bunch of kids in the Salvation Army hut. This stood at the end of Meavy Terrace in the quiet, almost sleepy rural village of Crownhill.

Just by looking back to that time and those days reminded me forcibly of some of the many changes that time and progress have brought about – reminiscing over old times is usually a pleasure, but added to that it's sometimes rather surprising just what you can come up with if you dig into the past. In any case a little bit of mind–bending research may prove of interest. The following story is a sample of the sort of domestic and social highlights which helped make up a Crownhill day nearly sixty years or so ago.

Magic Lantern Shows and some early Films

For those who may not know what a magic lantern was, that will be explained later, but, in the twenties generally it must be understood that most things in the entertainment world were in their infancy. If you listened to the wireless (if you could afford it!) when it first came about, it was through headphones (which hospitals and airliners use even now) but then it meant some experimental tinkering with a "cat's whisker" on a "crystal" (hence the old name "crystal set"). Try and explain that one to the kids, Grandpa! A horn–shaped loudspeaker (shades of *His Master's Voice)* which came next dispensed with the need for headphones and was obviously a great step forward as far as listening comfort was concerned; and from that time it wasn't long before the entire wireless set, even with the various combinations of wet and dry batteries and accumulators, was completely self–contained in the kind of cabinet we can still see today.

As regards the entertainment of a picture show in a viewing form the "magic lantern" – a "magical" thing it was indeed for us kids – was the very first to be presented. Crude enough as it may seem now it still is used in certain types of lectures to illustrate the subject in hand and was merely the art of showing a number of coloured slides in a lantern to project a picture on to a screen for viewing purposes.

Closely following on the heels of the magic lantern, with its allied amateurish hand waving "shadow graph" presentations, came the silent moving pictures (the "movies"). These carried visual dialogue in text form between film shots. The first of these "silent" film shows to arrive in Crownhill was given (by kind permission of the Army authorities) in a hut cinema which was situated at the corner of the Crownhill Barracks near to where the old Tamerton Cross (or corner) used to be. The films, a Cowboy entitled *Captian Jack and his Texas Rangers*, and a sort of Klu Klux Klan thriller called the *T-T-T's* (or something that sounded very much like that) were both serialised which meant that you were intended to come again. I'm sure that those films, and the later *Scotty the Scout* serial saga of the varied dangerous adventures of a troop of Boy Scouts achieved as strong a hold on us kids as ever did the *Fugitive* of a very much later T.V. audience.

In later years I ventured further afield and used to visit the Belgrave Cinema on Mutley Plain, Plymouth, to see the matinee show on a Saturday afternoon. For this outing my mother gave me threepence (3d) and it meant a walk of about a mile from Crownhill into Lower Compton where a tramride (½d each way) took me down to Mutley Plain. Admission to the Belgrave was a penny, that added to the tramfare left me with a penny to spend … it doesn't sound very much now but you'd be surprised just how many items you could get for a penny in those days. A whole "pennyworth" of sweets must have weighed a good quarter of a pound, that assorted bag was enough to last all through the matinee and half the way home!

The talking pictures or "the talkies", as they were colloquially known at first, were to come into general release around the 1930s, and I can remember my first called *Behind That Curtain* a detective–murder–mystery, which was shown (with tremendous queues resulting) at the Palladium Cinema in Ebrington Street in Plymouth.

But, I'm sure, the lack of sound never bothered us kids in the Belgrave as we clung to the edges of our seats during those cliff hanging "don't miss next week's episode" serials or

Tavistock Road, Crownhill

This early view of Tavistock Road, now Morshead Road, shows the post office on the corner of Alexandra Road which is now a chemist. Note the hedge on the right hand side, now a line of shops, and Spry's forge at the top standing out onto the road. Many of the present shops were then private houses and there were certainly no traffic problems in those days.

Widey Farm, pre-1914

This once well known local farm was part of the early Widey Court lands and is remembered being worked by Robert Stevenson and his family from about 1910 to about 1937. Other farmers were Dufty Bryant, 1889, and Samuel Kivel, 1902. Officers from the Barracks lodged at the farmhouse for a time and its cattle were often to be seen grazing land now covered with houses.

Beaumont Terrace, Saltash Road West

St. Nicholas's Hall, in the foreground, and most of the terrace houses were demolished and replaced by the subway complex in the 1960s. Two houses in the terrace were used as an orphanage next to Griffin's bakery. Now the only buildings left are Isbell's shop, the Methodist Church and 5 Crownhill Road. The houses overlooked the barrack parade ground.

Haymaking at Crownhill

So for us kids then it was the simple life with simple pleasures, like for instance, the hayrides when we rode out in haycarts from the village to the hayfields on various local farms where the hay, with the exception of some large heaps left for us kids to play on, was already gathered into hayricks. On these occasions you brought your own mug for tea, milk, or lemonade and, I can tell you, it was a very excited crowd of youngsters that assembled "up the village".

The bottoms of the haycarts would be well padded with hay when we clambered into them, but we still had a very bumpy ride that just about shook your teeth out especially when the wheels of haycarts rumbled into and out of the well worn cart ruts going through the gateways into the hayfields. But we enjoyed every minute of it all the same and when the drivers would stop their horses with the mighty "whoa!" out we would spill and away across the fields to the red and white marquees where our parents would be waiting to organise the sports and games. Later on came the refreshments and, what a time we would have in the hayfields then, diving into and tumbling over, being "buried" alive almost; having the skin rubbed red on your cheeks when "making hay", while the weather was always lovely and sunny, at least on looking back now, that's just how I remember it.

Day Trips in Wagonettes

As for those occasions such as the Chapel or Sunday School and Church Choir outings we used to ride out on the wagonettes. Now this was a sort of single or double decker horse–bus–cum–stage coach which could be drawn by two or four horses according to the size of the vehicle and the number of passengers carried. It will be appreciated that our trips in these wagonettes would only be for relatively short distances of about 10 or 15 miles and such places as Yealmpton, Shaugh Bridge, Mothecombe and Wembury became high on the list of our popular beauty spot venues.

It was the custom, on these wagonette trips, and a source of no little amusement for kids, that when we came to go up a hill on our journey for all the children and the younger folk to get out and walk. You can imagine probably just what that meant as like as not most of the kids would be over the hedges picking flowers, or apples, etc., according to the time and season and there, at the top of the hill, would be the parents and the drivers all yelling at the tops of their voices for us kids to hurry or "us'll never git there." (That's probably one of the reasons, apart from horse power, we didn't go far in those wagonettes).

A wagonette trip could also turn out to be rather a hazardous undertaking in those days as I can recall one particularly longer than usual (we must have started out before dawn) going to Seaton and Downderry in Cornwall. The weather on that day was unusually rough and windy so that when we began to climb up the coast road at Downderry the sight of the raging seas and near gale force wind so scared our horses that in the prancing around one of them went lame and had to be calmed down and taken into the nearest field to recover and rest up for a couple of days.

It was a case of all out of the wagonette and since curing a lame horse was not so easy as changing a wheel on a vehicle today, it meant that the passengers in our wagonette had to return home by train (to the added delight of us kids involved) from the St. German's Railway Station, whence we had been conveyed by my Uncle Bill's taxis from the old Mill Garage at Polbathic.

Horseless Carriages come to Crownhill

And now that I come to mention the word taxi I suppose there were cars of a sort about in those days, but I don't seem to remember seeing any around Crownhill for some appreciable length of time apart from the local doctor's conveyance.

My first real recollection of a motor vehicle was of one of those celebrated charabancs which arrived in the village via the Embankment Garage at Laira. This charabanc, (rough translation from the French, I believe, is *bancs* or rows of chars, chairs or seats) and the forerunner of today's modern coach. It was a huge brown and yellow monster that was open in design and had a folding canvas roof and side screens which could be raised in rough weather. The seats were placed in rows from side to side of the vehicle but there were no passageways down the middle for access; instead each row of seats had a door at each end so that with a charabanc with say eight rows of seats you had no less than sixteen door handles to play with and plenty of brasswork to polish!

But at least the charabancs did get a lot further than the wagonettes.

In the early days of the twenties things mechanical on the road were the exception rather than the rule. Where you can drive up to 40 m.p.h. through Crownhill today, in those days you could literally crawl across the same road on your hands and knees without disturbing the peace or the inhabitants. If you were so unfortunate as to get involved in a road accident it was a case then of being run down by a horse and cart. I distinctly remember my sister, Merle, having to have some stitches inserted after such an encounter.

The Village Fetes

High on the list of entertainments for us was the village fete which, pleasant thought, seems never to die out. The main one around Crownhill was usually held in the lovely grounds of Manadon House by kind permission of Major and Mrs. Hall–Parlby. People such as the Hall–Parlby's around the village had the common touch of the real gentlefolk, they simply did not know the meaning of 'sides', and I well remember the daughters at Manadon House, the Misses Blanche and Cynthia (both beauties at that), dancing quite happily with the local village gents at the Church room hop which was held often enough. Manadon House grounds were also the venue for the meet of the local foxhound pack.

Children used to be asked to assist at the running of various stalls at the fete, particularly if you happened to be a member of the Boy Scout or Girl Guide Companies and one felt a somebody, one who could be trusted with handling monies taken.

An amusing enough event at the fete used to be the vicar's tug–of–war event (a prize of apples for the winners) when it was quite usual for the abnormal number of pullers on each side to cause the rope to break and the rapid movements of competitors to opposite ends of the earth was a very common occurence.

An attraction for children at any village fete was the ice cream van. But today's children would have a job to recognise our hokey pokey man in his pagoda roofed, pony drawn, ice cream cart. But I'm sure they would have soon found him out by the sound of the huge leather handled bell he rang; while the brass pillars which supported the roof of his little square cart shone so beautifully you could have seen them a mile away.

I'd like to relate one little experience, amusing in an innocent way, which happened to me at one of our fetes. My mother had bought me a new red and white blazer for the event and off I went strutting proudly around like a peacock fully revelling in my get up. A sudden heavy shower of rain during the afternoon sent us scurrying for shelter and, I must admit, (such is the way of children) I got more than just a little bit damp in the process. It wasn't long before the sun came out again and we carried on with the fun but when I got home that day and took off my nice new blazer I found that my hitherto clean white shirt was completely covered with red and white stripes. Well I was petrified but mother just had to laugh even though she scolded me.

A feature of the fete at Manadon and at other such places was the high, sweeping swing fixed temporarily to one of the trees in the grounds. The seat of the swing was usually wide enough for two adults and at least three children to sit on and it took quite a lot of willing manpower to get you off the ground. But what a lovely view of things you would be rewarded with then when at the top of each swing.

One hears a lot about the swinging times we live in now; it strikes me that those (literally) were the real "swinging days". Everybody swung and even the popular songs raved about it. Anyway it was a cheap form of entertainment (it still is), it cost you nothing but a push to get you going and, as an exercise combined with pleasure, it was just the job.

But in our days of swinging, decorum had to have it's way as far as the ladies were concerned. A particular swinging ditty entitled, *Keep Your Skirts Down Nellie*, was very suitably illustrated on one visit our family made down to the Ash Tea Gardens at Saltash Passage. Mother had taken us for a jaunt–cum–tramride day out. At the Tea Gardens, where we enjoyed the same glorious views now enjoyed by thousands passing over and around the Tamar bridge, the usual swings were well in use but I noticed that the ladies were having their skirts tied modestly down either with a scarf, or an obliging gentleman's handkerchief, so as not to reveal (when being swung) any more than a fleeting glimpse of a well turned ankle, quite a contrast indeed from the very charming and revealing, mini skirt era of more recent years.

Trout's, the Crownhill Bakers

This business is now Stentifords but for many years it served the locality having taken over from the previous bakers, Colletts. This view of the shop and two ladies (does anyone recognise them?) was taken in the inter-war years. The boundary line between the parishes of St. Budeaux and Eggbuckland ran along the frontage of the shop the result being that the bakery was in St. Budeaux while the overhanging bay window was in Eggbuckland. The owners had to pay a shilling a year rent for the window!

"The Hole in the Wall Shop" 1928

Mrs. Pheobe Evans and her sister, Mrs. E. Cole, are here outside the small shop at the corner of Whitleigh Terrace. Sweets, cakes, bread, etc., were sold here and shop-made ice cream cooled with ice blocks from Brickwoods Ice factory collected on the bus! Wooden shutters were fitted into grooves to secure the windows each night.

A Carnival Entry

Here is the 1947 entry for the Tamerton carnival of George May's decorated vans used for his Crownhill butchers shop. Standing by them are Geoffery Floyd and his daughter, Eva, George Maker and Ben May, son. The business was at Morshead Terrace.

The annual School Sports

On the occasion of the annual school sports during the summer we children also had our moments to shine and show off our paces when dancing the Maypole which we had learnt so assiduously and, sometimes painfully, when Tommy Coombes the headmaster at Eggbuckland School caught us going the wrong way round in school breaks. The singing of, *Come Lassies and Lads, take leave of your Dads, and away to the Maypole High*, resounded across the sports ground, while the multi-coloured ribbons we weaved made a very pretty sight all fluttering in the summer breeze as you may well imagine.

Old time Morris dancing was also learnt in schools in our day but, believe me, our performing of *Gathering Peascods* (we children often used to wonder what on earth Peascods were) never achieved the heights of perfection, or pleasure, as did our glorious Maypole.

So it was simple pleasures for simple people in our day and, even our short rambles to Derriford, Whitleigh Hall and even Hartley Reservoir grounds via Linketty Lane became an adventure in itself. On these occasions mother's folded sunshade or parasol became a very handy receptacle for the lovely wild and sometimes not so wild, flowers that we might cull along the way.

Trips on the Water

Then as now we enjoyed the age old river trips from Admiral's Hard in Stonehouse or the Barbican cruising lazily up to Calstock, Weir Head, St. Germans or bobbing gently across to Jennycliffe. More daringly still and a special treat for the church choir, was a trip in a mackerel fishing boat out around the Breakwater or the Sound when we landed, often with queasy stomach, for a picnic-cum-barbicue on the beaches at Cawsand or Kingsand. From one of these trips I still retain a vivid picture in my mind of the time we passed under the lee of a towering man-o-war on the Tamar. The one I saw may have been the old H.M.S. *Impregnable* which was at that time being used as a training establishment. Her open gun ports were dotted with smiling young sailors who waved down boyishly to us from their lofty perches and, gazing up at the ship, it was easy to imagine that it was similar vessels which sallied forth to meet and destroy those mighty Spanish Armadas many, many years ago.

Around that time we children also had the novel excitement of a General Election and we had more than a bit of fun parading round the streets chanting songs in general support of a particular candidate. One main favourite ran, *Vote, vote, vote for (so and so) he's the man who's going to win*, and was sung to the tune of the, "Children of the World," chorus from the record disc, *Everything Is Beautiful In It's Own Way*. We would vary the names in our chantings to suit our respective political candidate. Maxwell Thornton, Liberal, was the popular man in the street choice, while the dashing Major Kenyon-Slaney, Conservative, who stood for the gentry and others who followed the Red, White and Blue, and Military and Naval traditions became the focus for your fancy.

For an indoor enjoyment on a wet afternoon or when one or other of us kids were sick in bed we enjoyed making pin pricked pictures from old magazine pages. Here you laid the page on the bed sheet or a blanket and pricked at the outline of the photo or picture with a large pin. This picture, when held up to the light (either of a lamp or window), would then appear to be illuminated with a myriad of little silver lights and could look quite entrancing, all for nothing at that.

Out on the roads we used to hitch rides on the back axles of pony carts and horsedrawn carriages amid the shouts of, "whip behind," by other kids and which would cause the driver to flick his whip around in no uncertain manner. This helped to pass many an hour during those leisurely country days.

Mr. Dugdale rides his Bicycle!

The first bicycle I ever remember seeing was also, in it's way, a bit of an event in the village and was certainly something of a diversion as far as I was concerned. It was the entertaining spectacle provided by quaint, good natured Mr. (?) Dugdale, Esq., the much respected piano tuner. I deliberately put the question mark for his christian name; but I'm sure it would have read something in the order of Theophilus or some distinguished name of that sort. Our knickerbocker clad Mr. Dugdale always travelled his country rounds on a bicycle but what form of propulsion he used to propel himself along since it wasn't always downhill with the wind behind, you were scarcely likely to find out. Our dear, quaint Mr. Dugdale was frequently seen to be free wheeling breezily along with his feet, like a schoolboy, perched precariously on the top of his bicycle's front forks!

Raymond's Corner
This well known Crownhill shop shows Mr. Roy Isbell standing with his father founder of the confectionery business. The building is known as *Beaumont House* and was formerly a saddlers run by A. Bowden.

Raymond's Corner
An early 1920s photograph shows why this is so called. The saddlery business served troops stationed in Crownhill Barracks and here one military man is sporting what was then the latest model bicycle. Infantry Regiments were stationed at Crownhill and during the First World War considerable numbers of horses were there as well.

Tavistock Road, Crownhill
The shops in the 1930s with a notable absence of traffic. The buildings still look much the same but the names have changed. Then it was T. M. Beswick, general leader and Reeves fish and chip shop, the closure of which was regretted by many local people.

Apart from his spectacle on a bike it was really more than something of a show to listen to his astounding musical repertoire on the occasions when he came to tune our piano. This was always a mixture of classical and popular musical items; he must have been more than a bit of a Paderewski in his way, and his reverberating crescendos of ascending and descending octaves certainly made the old anti–macassars swing and dance in our front room.

A Family Outing

Then there was the summer when our family enjoyed the surprising luxury of being driven out to Yelverton and Dousland in an open carriage for pleasant picnics and tea on the grass and, later in the autumn, for a longer drive out to the Goose Fair at Tavistock. On that occasion I remember I would insist on riding outside on the box with the coachman. But I can tell you now that it was a very near frozen little bundle who got lifted down at Yelverton and had to be thawed out with hot milk in the warm interior of the coach before we proceeded further.

These somewhat expensive excursions, I suspect now, were paid for out of my father's gratuity received when he eventually retired from general service with the Somerset Regiment with whom he did a full–time stretch, including ten year's stay in India (that's what you call overseas service). That's what the Army meant in those British Empire days. Mine was a comparative "Cook's Tour" when I went out to India at a much later date.

During the colder weather or on wet or indeterminate evenings my mother used to entertain us kids around the fire in the parlour with dialect stories about Jan Stewer and Widecombe Fair. "Caw they wudden' aff' broad, though." Country bred as we may have been those amusing tales had more often than not to be "translated" for our benefit since, "Well us cudden' unnerstand' aff' on it, could us?"

A local Celebrity of the Village

In her own way I suppose my mother was something of a local celebrity. She used to play the piano and sing at the local concerts. She also used to play more or less regularly the organ in the Garrison Church in Crownhill keeping the choir (of whom I was a member) in tune and order as well. She officiated and participated at local whist drives and dances. She "helped" me to dance in later years dragging me out on the floor to learn by the scruff of my neck something for which I'll always thank her since I later enjoyed the benefits of being able to dance at the local village hops and farmers' balls.

Mother was also involved with the Mothers' Union and local Guilds. She had travelled abroad with my father during his tours after the First World War. Malta and China were among the countries she visited. She was game for anything and was bold and forthright; poor old Dad was quiet and unassuming. I particularly remember her fine rendering of the Irish song, *Killarney*, at a concert being held in the old Buffalo Lodge Hall (where my father was a member) which was then situated at the rear of the Tamar Hotel in Crownhill. Sitting low in my seat I responded with a mixture of boyish admiration and a kind of embarassment (natural I suppose) at seeing my mother perform in public.

Widey Court and its alleged Ghost

She also used to regale us with extremly interesting tales of "upstairs and downstairs" life in the big houses of those days. Her own mother had served as a housekeeper after working her way up through the ranks of servant girl, tweeny maid and other more exalted positions before reigning more or less supremely in the general household. So my mother had plenty to draw on for stories repeated for our interest in that context as also the stories of local legends. One story I remember concerned nearby Widey Court, an estate near the village from whence came the spine chilling tale of a headless coachman who, at some stage of the moon or other such time would be seen to be driving a ghostly carriage past the Court at midnight. With bated breath we kids would listen to the story and could easily imagine the terrible fate which would befall the unfortunate individual who would dare to look upon the horrifying spectacle. It was also rumoured a member of the nobility was once hidden in a secret chamber on the side of the grand staircase of the house. Was he a cavalier on the run from the Roundheads in Cromwell's day? What with Prince Rupert's close association with the area near Trematon Castle on the nearby river Tamar we have a goodly share of historical interest. In fact, unless my memory deceives me, to almost having a King Charles oak tree somewhere in the vicinity.

It was also told to us and was reputed to be true of a pet parrot belonging to an old Inn at

Tavistock Road, Crownhill

The village seen from the crossroads well before 1900. Isbell's shop on the corner has yet to be built. This building was used as a general meeting place and as a law court at some stage in its history. Spry's forge window juts on the left which bordered Hobson's field where villagers enjoyed themselves on various festive days.

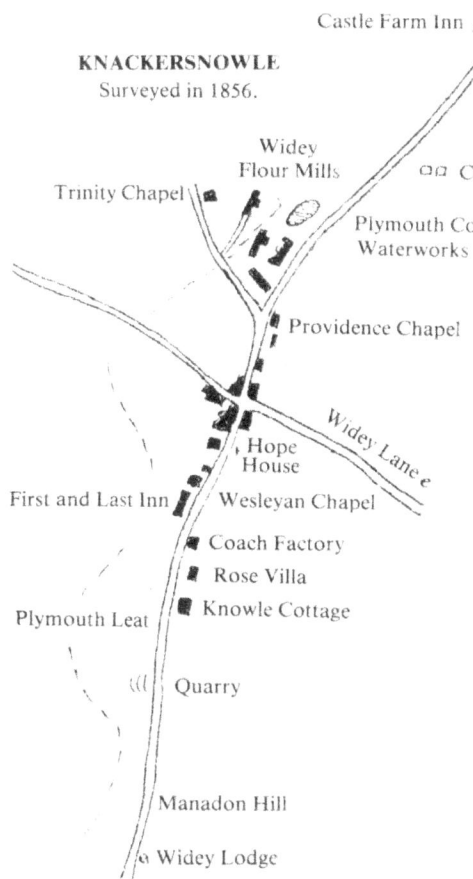

KNACKERSNOWLE
Surveyed in 1856.

J. D. Davey, general dealer

This dates from the first decade of this century and shows the staff of the shop which is now the Co-op. Mrs. Davey is seen here with her daughters, Lilian, Tempe and Ida. The business was later run by the Beswicks, then Dingles from Plymouth after which came the Co-op.

Antony Passage (also on the Tamar). This parrot appeared to be famed far and wide for his ripe old English language but, sad to relate, was one day blown into the river by a boisterous wind, drowned and then mourned by all and sundry. Mother's stories also included the legend and curse of Mount Edgcumbe House but, to me, that story is of a personal nature and will remain untold here.

Local Football Matches

She also followed sports and football matches as such and it used to be the practice in the season on Saturday afternoons to place the flowers on the altar in the Garrison Church ready for the Sunday services and for us to walk out to the Army football grounds near Bowden Cross and Eggbuckland Fort where we enjoyed the amateurish but very wholehearted displays of the locally based Army football teams. We once witnessed a very thrilling Army Cup semi-final at that ground (I think one of the teams was the South Staffordshire's) but the football, believe me, was of a very high standard indeed; in fact more than quite a few of the Army football stars of those days were bought out by the professional football teams. I believe Nobby Cromptom, later of Arsenal, was one of these stars.

As regards this I can also clearly remember my mother taking me to Home Park to see Argyle. I can just about remember exactly where we were standing opposite the main stand and the star of the day for me and no doubt the crowd, was Welsh international, Moses Russell, who always seemed to be very much in the public eye as was Fred Craig the more than somewhat temperamental goalkeeper on the Argyle's books at that time. I was about ten years of age at the time and there was nearly a riot on the terraces when Fred Craig fed up to the teeth with Moses Russell having stopped everything coming his way and thereby stopping him from getting his name in the *Football Herald,* folded his arms, leant against the nearer post, and deliberately let a soft ball which Moses Russell had gratuitously given him trickle into the net. But those, of course, were the halcyon days of the old Southern League. A pity, in some ways, that those carefree footballing days seem to be gone for ever.

Derriford House and Farm

But in the main those days' simple pleasures would come in simple guises and one came for us at Sunday School where it was the custom in fine weather for the boys to escort home our Sunday School teacher who lived up in one of the big houses at Derriford. I'm sure we boys all had that pure boyish crush for our teacher who certainly, to us, had everything – charm, good looks and breeding, judging by the beautiful house she lived in. Our reward, after that lovely intimate stroll up the pleasant driveway to the big house, was her radiant smile of thanks, some flowers to take home or several choice apples from the ripening racks for our immediate consumption.

My father worked up at Derriford after his discharge from the Army for "crusty" Squire Ratcliffe on his Derriford estate where he looked after a small herd of Jersey cows kept specially for the exclusive use of the Derriford household. My father was also a general handyman on the estate. He had undertaken a course in carpentry; repaired all the gates as well as milking the cows which used to follow him around like sheep. His reward, on top of his wages, was a quart of milk each day and a large pot of solid scalded cream on Sundays. In his spare time, like most men in the village, he helped in all the hay-field operations gathering in the hay at the Widey and Whitleigh farms. We kids and all always enjoyed the end of harvest feast held in the farmhouse barn (tweren't nuff room in the kitchen, wuzz't) when huge, cold rounds of beef and ham were carved and served with cold spuds and salads with home made bread and farm butter to help it all down. Barrels of beer and cider on tap were available for the men while we children (who'd helped in the fields when the hay was gathered) had glasses of milk and, on top of all the foregoing, we always looked for that lovely slab of dough cake made by the farmers' wives (out of sour milk my mother used to tell us, apart from other ingredients) anyway it was delicious.

On the occasion of really warm weather when gathering in the hay in summertime, it was a great delight to help drink my father's cold tea. This was made in the house, cooled, milked and sweetened and then "bottled". The bottles were then placed in a running stream at the side of the hayfield to keep cool and you may imagine how refreshing that wonderful concoction was.

Hoops and Wooden Tops for the Kids

During the seasons we kids enjoyed a number of varied amusements among them hoops.

Saltash Road West

This country view of Crownhill shows the main Saltash Road flanked by open fields of Brake Farm. This is now the dual carriageway and housing estates cover much of the land. The former Haroldsleigh Terrace is on the left, one building being used as a general store by Mrs. Doris Hatherleigh. The present day fire station is situated opposite.

Beaumont Terrace

This photograph was taken around the turn of the century and shows the line of the Old Crownhill Road leading to Meavy Avenue. The houses went in 1968 for the flyover scheme but one has remained as a reminder of this area. On the left is the railings and gate of the early Methodist Chapel and opposite was the barrack square area.

Saltash Road East

This is now known as Fort Austin Road the houses of which then faced the well known Plumer Barracks. These were demolished in the 1960s and government offices stand on the site. Although the road has changed the houses and buildings in the distance will still be recognised. Who is the person standing in the road?

These were first made out of wood, but as they used to break fairly easily it was not long before we had the local blacksmith, Mr. Bill Tapp, to fashion us some iron ones which we happily "ran" and pursued around the place, at times arduously, trundling them all the way from Crownhill down to Eggbuckland school where we parked them like bikes in a corner of the school playground.

Then we had wooden tops which we spun with small whips to see who could keep them spinning the longest, covering sometimes a fair distance as we did so. Conkers, still popular today, were also high on the list of diversions in the autumn, while cigarette cards and cigarette packet collections were all the rage. My uncles, being officers in the Navy came in very useful for cigarette card collections, saving as they did their cards for me from their tobacco issue while away on their service overseas.

Money and Locally grown Food

As regards money in our days I suppose you could say that most families were in rather tight or at least straightened circumstances although there did not seem to be much unemployment around. As regards to food we were indeed very well off. All vegetable and agricultural produce came from well manured gardens, allotments and fields. Bread, for instance, was really worth eating and, coupled with local farm butter, could be almost a meal in itself. We kids had strictly to take our turn as to who got the crusts off a loaf, while the "tuff cakes", a sort of breadroll, literally melted in your mouth.

I suppose meals in general followed more or less the same routine menus as today, but I can particularly remember with relish the delicious bubble and squeak which on Mondays regularly followed Sunday's roast. Now as regards that Sunday dinner it was the practice on Sunday mornings for mother to take the prepared dinner in its dish across the field behind our house up to the local baker who, after the early morning's bread had been baked, used to pop any such prepared dinner dishes in the back of the huge oven where it would remain until cooked shortly before dinner time. This most helpful service used to cost our mothers as much, or as little, as a penny and the aroma which hovered around the snow white, cloth covered dish as Mam carried it back home assailed our very nostrils and awaiting stomachs.

You could always reckon fish to be in a freshly caught condition. Our local fishmonger, George Damerell, used to drive a flat pony cart out from the Barbican to Crownhill and his fish were really "alive, alive, oh!". Their tails used to be still flapping when you bought them.

Belt-driven Motorcycles, the Circus and R101

I have mentioned the fact that it was a very rare sight to see a motor vehicle on the roads in our days. While on the subject I think the earliest ones I remember seeing are worthy of some mention. Motor bikes were belt driven machines with wide, spreading handlebars (like the horns of a wild west steer), while their petrol tanks must have been provided by some manufacturer of cocoa tins or the like and they were capable of speeds of about 12 miles an hour downhill with the wind behind them! It was a very common sight to see two passengers being carried on their pillions and on top of that there were no helmet regulations, the only concession to clothing for the head was a pilot type helmet usually crowned with a pair of goggles to help keep the dust and any gnats out of the wearer's eyes.

Among other very uncommon sights we used to see in our boyhood days was the highly exciting "sky writing" advertising performed by light acrobatic planes and also the rare visits of Sir Alan Cobham's *Flying Circus*. This was a great show at the then Roborough Polo Ground where I remember leading some polo ponies into, and which was then being used as a landing field for light aircraft. I can also remember that it was on the occasion of the Flying Show that I was able to have my first flight in an open cockpit plane over Crownhill and Plymouth at a cost, maybe somewhat extravagant in those days, of 5 shillings, now 25p, and which you could reckon on being worth about a sixth of a weeks wages!

Later on, probably not quite in boyhood times, we also experienced the marvellous spectacle the airship, R101, as it cruised over Plymouth one bright summer afternoon. In more than one way those were really exciting times we lived in then – having gone to the moon seems somehow very remote (and unimportant) today.

The Prince of Wales pass through Crownhill

For us kids also there came that very grand and glorious occasion in, I think, 1919 when we all lined the Crownhill main village street to see the fabulous being, the Prince of Wales, who passed through on his way from Tavistock into Plymouth in an open carriage. I can't really say that I actually saw him, except that I do remember hearing someone say, "Oh look, there

Crownhill Junior A.F.C. 1921-22

This jubilant group shows the champions of this league for Plymouth. In it are Mr. Frank Wills, Les Ellacott, Bill Drake, Stan Ellacott, Bill Evans, Bill Smith, Steve Short, Ron Boney, Bill Waterworth, Frank Wills, Wilf Stribley, Harry Bartlett and others. The whole team were Crownhill boys.

Cricket at Crownhill

This photograph was loaned by a local person but only a Mr. Priest has been identified in it. The team had a very good following in those days and sported a number of local enthusiasts in gaining success in more matches at home than away.

Crownhill Juniors A.F.C. 1922-23

The board of medals and cups tell yet another story of success for this local team of youngsters. Fred Cutland, Wilfrid Stribley, Bill Evans, Charlie Hansford, Mr. Skentlebury, Mr. W. Evans, Bill Kingwell, Frank Wills and others have been identified here.

he is." We all waved our little flags madly having received a day off from school for the occasion and each bore proudly home a beautiful mug so lavishly inscribed with all the members of the Royal Family to hang up on the kitchen dresser for a short posterity.

Donkey Rowe of Crownhill

Another source of pleasure or at least an entertainment of sorts which we kids and grown ups used to take part in, was the happening (for want of a better word) at the Tamar Cross or Corner which I've mentioned earlier in this story. Tamerton Cross then carried a kind of notoriety in that it was the spot where a character known as *Donkey* Rowe used to hold his open air religious services. Mr. or *Donkey* Rowe, as he was popularly called, was quite an amusing and startling phenomenon to see or listen to. He sported a huge white beard and straw hat and with his staff in his hand strongly resembled an old time prophet as he paraded up and down his beat haranging all and sundry who happened to be passing or listening to him with his pointed and highly flavoured orations.

Donkey Rowe in his working life had about eight or nine donkeys, which is obviously how he got his name. All tethered one behind each other they used to pull donkey carts all the way from Honicknowle village via Crownhill over to Whitleigh Woods where he used to gather logs and firewood from fallen trees, a concession I presume from the Squire of Whitleigh Hall. These daily expeditions used to take *Donkey* Rowe nigh all day, sometimes almost to evening, to accomplish and was achieved through much berating and belabouring of his stubborn "mokes". His blaring, vociferous voicings of oaths and curses he used on his charges used to resound over the fields from Whitleigh to Crownhill and scare the crows for miles around. It really was no mystery at all why he became so famous for his oratories at his services at Tamerton Cross since his lecturings on his intelligent donkeys ensured him of plenty of practice for his human audiences.

That *Donkey* Rowe could orate was definitely not at all a debatable point, in fact it was a job to stop him once he got going as testifies the following humorous little bit of dialogue, the like of which used to enliven the proceedings at the Cross. A member of his flock, no doubt thinking of opening time at the Tamar Hotel or something of that sort, suddenly cut into *Donkey* Rowe's efforts with a rather loud and significant, "Amen", to which our prophet – highly resenting this not so naive interruption – retorted, "Taint Amen yet, my friend." Poor *Donkey* Rowe got no change out of that however when back came the stark rejoinder, "No! well it b..... well ought to be, then." I'm smiling even now remembering, but that sort of event certainly helped to entertain and sometimes to bring down the curtain for all our benefits or I'm sure we'd have been there all night.

I help at a Magic Lantern Show

Now I come to the *piece de resistance,* so to speak, of this story and a magic lantern show in the little hut one used to see from Raymond's Corner in Crownhill which for me almost was the main cause of all this "yurr rememberin business." When the magic lantern show eventually arrived in Crownhill it was first shown at the old Salvation Army hut which was situated at the end of Meavy Terrace where we kids, after paying our h'pennies for admittance were crammed into our seats noisily awaiting the show, on that magical apparatus the magic lantern. But, after the usual comings and goings, it became obvious that owing to some reason or other there was going to be a delay. We kids eventually fell silent wondering after all whether the show might be put off. We then learned from the local vicar, who mounted the stage whereon was erected a large white bed sheet used as a screen, that as the magic lantern operator's assistant had not turned up they were hoping to find a substitute from the audience. "Substitute volunteer?" what did that mean we wondered? Then the vicar turned to speak to one of our school teachers who was also on the stage and then seemed to be satisfied about something judging by the smile on his face. He came down off the stage and along the aisle towards the row where I was sitting. He bent down and whispered something to the boy at the end of the row which I could almost instinctively feel was meant for my hearing. I began to feel rather apprehensive. Was I being sent home? Had something happened which was to cause me to miss this wonderful show? "The vicar wants you Billie" (for some reason I was called Billie after a favourite uncle). I heard the voice as being far away but, feeling pretty awful, I got up and scrambled out of the row to where the vicar was waiting, with a broad smile right across his face. "Don't be alarmed, Billie," he said reassuringly. "Everything is all right." He could tell by the look on my face I was anxious about missing the show. The vicar called for order while holding on to me firmly, "Quiet please, children," he said. "I have to tell you that the magic lantern operator's assistant hasn't turned up and as a result I am going to ask Billie, who as you may know is a very good reader in school (this may have been true I realised later but a bit of flannel for all that) to read the stories while the operator shows the magic lantern slides."

So that's what I had to do I thought as I found myself being ushered down the hall to the magic lantern stand where the operator smiled and said "sit on this high chair Billie, you'll be able to read the book by the light from this little window in the side of the lantern and I'll tell you when to start."

I held the book of stories shakily in my hands as the operator began to insert the first lantern slide and then, "now Billie," he instructed softly, "start reading". I began to read, I suppose successfully enough, because at the end of the story I was given an enthusiastic reception which really made my day. I felt like a dog with two tails, something I've never experienced again in my life. I really felt I was part of that magic lantern, and in a way too you could almost say that was my first "Talkie" and in that little Salvation Army hut which once stood across from Raymond's Corner.

Yes, they were happy days then (I suppose they always are when you're young) but, so much for our hay rides, our maypoles, our wagonettes and all that, and dear old colourful *Donkey* Rowe with his pulpit the length of a sentry beat. They were as much of the country village which helped make up our image of that era more than half a century ago buried now beneath the march of time, progress and the new Crownhill flyover.

Manadon Hill in 1946

This post-war view of the main road shows that it consisted of a single carriageway at the bottom of which buses had to wait to pass each other. Note the water fountain on the left, Widey Lodge, to the right, and the dense trees overlooking the hill.

Crownhill Junior School about 1937

This smiling group of local children with their teacher will no doubt bring back memories to people who attended the school during this decade. Kenneth Charlton, Buster Stephens, Pat Jury, Dennis Baxter, Bill Hansford have been recognised but not the others or the teacher. Do you know them?

Tamar Hotel Outing

This outing is thought to date from the early 1920s and is said to be the first ever coach trip from the newly-built hotel. The char-a-banc, with its full length hood, was crowded for the occasion and hopefully will bring back memories from those days.

Crownhill Football Team

This group photograph dates from the early 1920s and includes Wilfrid Stribley, Mr. Skentlebury, Fred Cutland, Bill Evans, Bill Waterworth, Bill Kingwell, Steve Short, Harry Bartlett and Frank Wills with other lads from Plymouth.

Some Local People

Mr. W. Evans and his son, Bill, on the motor bike, are seen outside of Mrs. Evans' shop in Whitleigh Terrace about 1928 while to the left the old Guinness advert is taken up by William C. Hansford as part of a local procession in the middle 1930s. Members of St. Budeaux parish council are grouped below of whom Mr. W. Remfry, Mr. C. Hansford, Mr. E. Willcock, Mr. J. Pengelly, Mr. H. F. Davey, Mr. T. Thomas and Mrs. E. M. Cook represent Crownhill.

The Tamar Inn, Crownhill

This very early picture shows the former inn and main road sometime before 1900. A certain William H. M. Cudlip was listed as a "beer retailer" here in 1888 and no doubt many a traveller going to Tavistock would stop here for refreshment and rest for his horse. The inn and adjacent building were demolished to make way for the present Tamar Hotel, although the building behind the horse and cart still stands as Davis's Garage. It was once a corn and forage merchants store, then a Dame School and originally a chapel. Spry's forge is at the top of the road. The view below of the inn is looking south towards Plymouth and was probably taken on the same occasion as the one above. Some of the people look as though they are in both photographs. A much better view of the old cottages probably recalls one of the earliest pictures ever taken of the then "Knackersnowle" hamlet. These buildings were gone by 1900 and their occupants and uses now long forgotten.

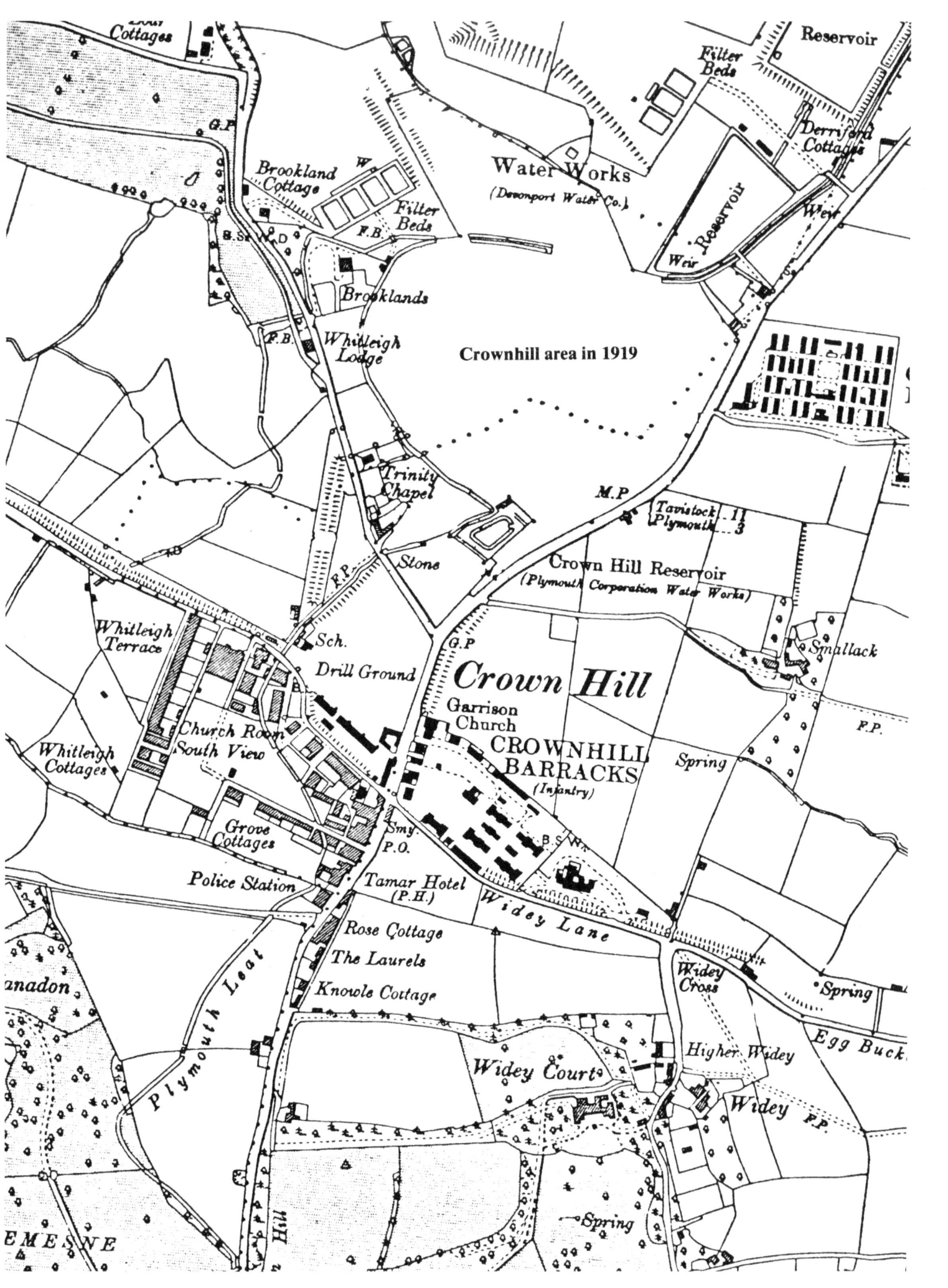

Shops and Tradesmen at Crownhill

These three pictures show the owners and helpers of just one village shop which was in business as shown here from 1940 to about 1965. It was previously owned by Mr. Ponsford who had kept the nearby Tamar Hotel and then sold to Mr. and Mrs. Evans. These photographs are of the 1950s when it was run by Mrs. Jane Bowman and helped in the evening by her husband, seen below. Troops returning to Crownhill each evening found the hot drinks and pasties which were for sale a convenient supper on their way to the barracks. The shop remained open until midnight after the last bus had arrived from town.

Employer and Staff

This pleasant group comprises of Mr. and Mrs. J. Bowman with their son, George, on the right with the shop staff in the early 1950s.

Some other Shopkeepers

A look through the trade directories since the turn of the century will show that many people have had businesses in this area. Charles Collett, baker, is given in 1888 then S. Collett in 1903. Thomas Coombe was a tailor, Thomas Heard, a shopkeeper, William Lacey, dairyman, H. Bickell, builder, Miss Bradford, dressmaker, J. Easdon, photographer, E. Hortop, dairy, W. Naylor, general shop and Robert Stevenson, baker and many others.

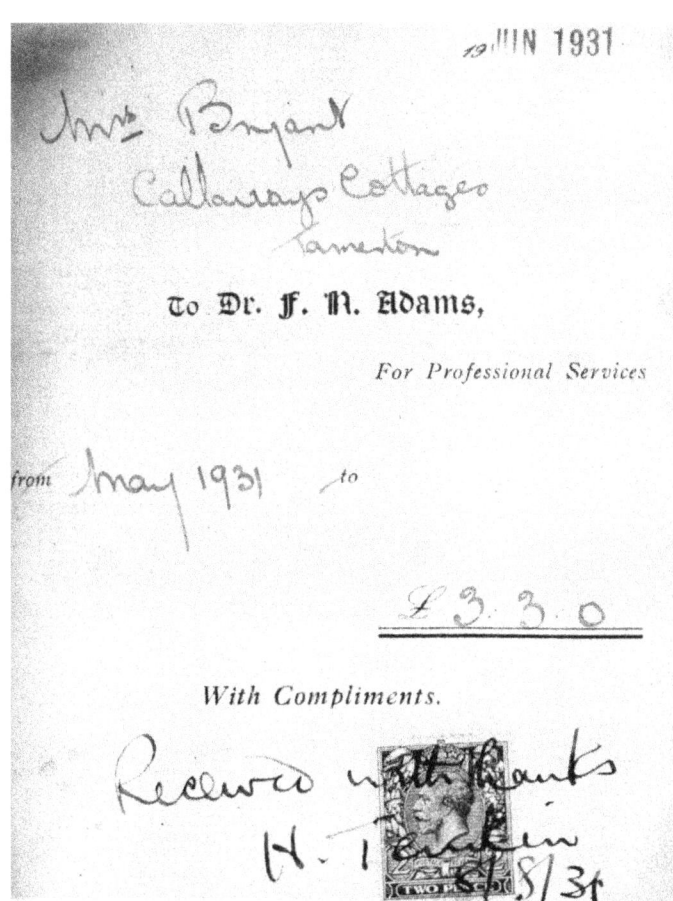

Doctor's Bill

Crownhill and area have been served for many years by Dr. Adams and above is a receipt for the safe delivery of a child at Tamerton in 1934. It is signed by H. Temkins who was the doctor in attendance. The doctor and nurse De Vaney who used to live in the small houses called Crownhill Villas.

Boundary Stones

These two stones are still in position on Manadon Hill defining part of the boundary between the parishes. The word *Tything* refers to a tenth of an area of land upon which tithes were formerly payable.

Crownhill Shops sometime before 1910

These shops are houses now, forming the main shopping area for Crownhill and are named after the Morshead family who lived in Widey Court for many years following the Civil War in the 1640s. None of the people shown have been recognised. Who were the riders in the pony and traps? Charles Collett had the bakery before Trouts, higher up is Daveys, the general dealers, and further still is the butchers shop owned in turn by J. H. Willcocks, G. Denley, 1914 to 1926, R. H. Rickman and then George May.

Crossroads, Crownhill

This 1930s view of the main crossroads had to give way to the present road system because of the notorious bottle-necks here. The road going from left to right is the dual carriageway without, of course, the traffic lights as seen here. Lucke's Garage stands on the site of Spry's forge while the right hand shop is still run by the Isbell family.

KNACKERSNOWLE (CROWNHILL) in 1888

Post Office: John Norsworthy, postmaster. Letters received by foot messenger at 7 a.m., despatched 12.30 p.m. and 5.40 p.m. and on Sundays at 10.50 a.m. via Plymouth, the nearest Money Order Office. There is a wall letter box at Honicknowle cleared at 5.00 p.m. weekdays and at 10.45 a.m. Sundays.

Chapel: Wesleyan.
Assistant overseer: William Fairweather, Whitleigh Terrace.
Income tax collector: James Butland, Coombe Farm, Honicknowle.

Private residents:
Barlow, J., Whitleigh Terrace
Crocker, Mrs. M., 5 Whitleigh Terrace
Durant, Mrs. M. J., 4 Whitleigh Terrace
Ingkis, Mrs. Agnes, 19 Whitleigh Terrace

Commercial:
Bragg, Albion, refreshment house
Collett, Charles, baker
Coombe, Thomas, tailor
Cudlip, W. H. M., beer retailer
Davey, Francis, shopkeeper
Fairweather, Wm., senior, rate collector
Goodyer, James, lodging house
Langford, Edwin Chase, surgeon
Heard Thos. C., shopkeeper
Hodge, W. G., nurseryman
Nicholls, Richard, jobbing gardener
Nosworthy, John and Son, saddlers and Post Office
Passmore, Wm. and Son, coach builders
Pengelley, George, wheelwright
Raymond, Hy. Wmm., *New Inn*
Royal Engineers' Office
Treneman, Wm., mason and builder
Wyatt, Mrs. Annie, butcher, etc.

Old Police Station

The village from the top of Manadon Hill looking north with the former Police station in the centre which stood next to the library. Both went in the new road scheme. Trelawney House, left foreground, also went together with many once familiar scenes and other buildings.

Tavistock Road

This pre-1914 scene shows the rural atmosphere of the higher part of Crownhill. Two kilted soldiers are walking by land upon which was later built the Masonic Hall. Note the side road going up to Crownhill Fort.

Crownhill Fort

This very large limestone fortification was built during the 1860s as part of a defensive system of encircling Plymouth with two rings, an outer and inner, against an anticipated attack by Napoleon. This, of course, never came and the forts have not been used in anger. Lord Palmerston authorised their construction and because of high costs they were dubbed "Palmerston's Follies" by local people.

Trinity Church

Built in 1843 as a Chapel of Ease at a cost of £538, troops were marched down to it from Crownhill Fort for service each week. The larger Garrison Church became more popular and eventually Trinity ceased as a place of worship. Cyril Crossman is remembered as its organist and it had a choir of local boys. It was then used as a youth club at the time of the last war and is now a store for the city library.

Widey Court

These two photographs show the mansion as remembered sometime before the last war and then as a partial ruin a few years before its demolition in 1953.

Civil War Times

The house and grounds were used as the headquarters of the Royalists who laid siege to the citizens of Plymouth during the early 1660s but without success. They were led by Sir Richard Grenville. Prince Rupert visited the headquarters and Charles I is reputed to have spent some time in the house.

The last years of Widey Court

Part of the house was let out to tenants and here a group pose for the camera in 1942. They are Ruth Frowde, Mrs. Margaret Frowde, Lilia Northey Frowde, Joan Frowde, Jean Frowde and the baby, Christopher Frowde. The husband of Margaret was Benjamin who was the resident police sergeant here when the house was used by the city police. Widey was in the ownership of the Morshead family up until the 1870s then a Commander and Mrs. Davy were given as the next occupants. Various changes took place over the years until it was requisitioned by Plymouth in 1941 and used by the police until 1945 when it was then used as a store. Rooms were let to private tenants, the last leaving the grand old building in March, 1950. A compulsory order was put on it and the lands for development by Plymouth and bulldozers tore the building asunder during 1953–4 so bringing to an end one of Plymouth's famous and colourful mansions.

Barrack Gates, Crownhill

The barracks were built 1891–92 and this early picture shows the main entrance in about 1920 when they were known as *Plumer Barracks*. The entrance to the Garrison Church is just beyond the gates and to the Sergeants' mess. Above this is the old British Legion or village hall club facing the old road to Tavistock.

Officers' Mess, the Barracks

This elegant, ivy-covered building was the officers' mess and part residential quarters for junior officers. Senior ranks lived out but they all used this building not only for dining purposes but for many grand social occasions as well. It was one of the last buildings to go here having been of more recent years used as a Magistrates Court. The photograph is pre-1914.

Scotsmen at Crownhill

This group of soldiers was part of the very large contingent of men stationed at Crownhill from where they were marched, with band ahead, down to Plymouth on their way to France in 1914. Their kilted comrades were once a popular sight in the area. The Royal Scots and Highlanders both had distinctive uniforms.

The Guardroom and Entrance

These are seen here leading into Crownhill Barracks at the turn of the century. Troops were allowed out in uniform only after checking themselves against a large wall mirror affixed to the outside of one of the cell walls on the left of this scene.

Old Tamerton Foliot Road

Later accommodation blocks for military men were built on the west side of Tavistock Road. Here this open view shows part of them with the bath house to the left. The foreground area was later built upon. This scene is thought to be around 1910.

Meavy Avenue and Alexandra Road

Residents gather at the gate of one of the many houses shortly to be demolished for the flyover. The back of the post office is on the left in Alexandra Road, once known in part as Stoke Terrace. Meavy Avenue is to the left in this photograph.

Beaumont Place, 1960s

Another part of Crownhill which went when the flyover road scheme was developed in the late 1960s. The back of Griffin's bakery is on the left, the two ladies are walking in the area of the new flyover and all the houses shown are now gone.

Meavy Avenue, 1960s

Part of this avenue still stands, the right side, which runs parallel to the new main Tavistock road. Alexandra Road runs at right angle to Meavy Avenue at the bottom here although most of these houses have gone as well. The new road scheme brought about dramatic changes to this part of the village.

Wesleyan Soldiers, Home

This was founded during the First World War as an extension of the "Welcome" Soldiers and Sailors Home, Devonport. "Tiny" Williams was the manager. There was a refreshment bar, concert hall, recreation and reading rooms for the troops stationed in the large garrison and a chaplain was at hand. The building is now the Manadon Masonic Hall.

Char-a-banc Outing

This 1923-24 photograph shows many of the boys who played in the local football team about to set off for the day from Crownhill on what was probably the annual treat. Archie Stribley and his wife have been recognised on the coach. No doubt many others will be easily named by friends.

Pascho, Newsagent and Tobacconist

Here can be seen some of the Crownhill shops at the turn of the century with Paschos showing the long barber's pole (a barber worked at the back of the old shop), a dog waits patiently outside Colletts, the bakers, and the pony and traps stand outside the Post Office then ran by Mr. Thomas Coombe who also was a tailor.

The Crossroads
This view of the main road and lights was taken a few months prior to the major developments of 1968 and shows the main road going towards Saltash. The corner shop is still there but Beaumont Terrace has gone except the nearest house. A once familiar area that went all too suddenly for the flyover.

Whitleigh Avenue
Taken from Crownhill Road two little girls enliven this scene playing hockey in the road. Buildings cover the right hand side and coals are no longer available from the corner house.

Meavy Avenue
Shadows fall along this avenue on houses shortly to be demolished in the late 1960s. The hall at the top of the road stood with its small cross on the roof. This was St. Christopher's Hall, one time village hall and used for many organisations and events.

Crownhill Fort Area

These two post-war photographs show Crownhill as most residents still remember it. The very large limestone fort dominated the higher ground for many years and was then surrounded by open land. Much of this has now been developed but here can be seen the open reservoir, the filter beds above and to the right of the fort, open fields, below left, now covered by houses in Elgin Cresent and other roads.

Built up Crownhill

This aerial view shows the city side of the village after considerable housing developments which took place during the 1930s. The thin arm of part of Widey lands breaks into the houses reaching the main road to the left. Cross Park Way and other adjacent roads cover the fields shown in the picture on the cover of this book which was taken in 1927.

Arthur L. Clamp – the man behind the books

Arthur Leslie Clamp was a man of boundless energy with a passion for helping others, particularly through his love of history. A printer by trade, he started his career in a printing company before moving his family from Exeter to Plymouth to teach at the Plymouth College of Art and Design, where he eventually became the Head of the Printing Department.

A Devoted Family Man

Arthur with his five children.

Despite his love of teaching, Arthur prioritised his family, always making it home by 5:30pm for tea. He and his wife, Rosemary, raised five children: Susan, Angela, Elizabeth, David, and Steven. Arthur would often combine his love of family and history by taking his children on Sunday walks, encouraging them to appreciate historical monuments by taking photos or making crayon rubbings of gravestones for his books. The family home at 203 Elburton Road was a hub of activity, with a large garden, featuring a two-storey fort and a makeshift swimming pool.

A Lifelong Learner and Adventurer

Arthur's thirst for knowledge extended beyond history to a deep curiosity about the world. He was passionate about exploring different cultures, traditions, and cuisines, often taking advantage of his long summer holidays as a teacher to travel to places like India, Russia, South America, the middle east and the USA, sometimes bringing one of his children along. This adventurous spirit even influenced his home life, as seen by the short-lived family tradition of steam-cooking vegetables after a trip to Iceland.

History is a prominent feature of family days out

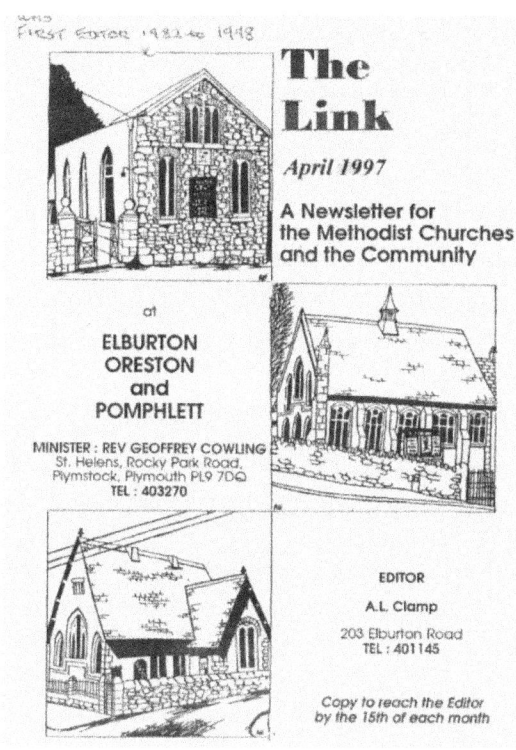

Community and Philanthropic Spirit

His commitment to serving others was evident in his long-standing involvement with the Elburton Methodist Church. He was the Sunday School Superintendent for over 15 years and served as the editor of the wider church's monthly newsletter, "The Link," for a similar duration. After Rosemary's very sad passing, Arthur later remarried and, following a chance encounter with a professor from India, established a connection with a missionary school in Chennai. Together with his new wife, Christine, he co-founded a "Sponsor a Child's Education" program that continues to this day.

*Pictured left – The cover of 'The Link' complete
with hand drawn sketches of each church by Angela
Below right – Arthur Clamp promoting his latest book
Below left – Arthur at home with his first wife, Rosemary
Below centre – Arthur on holiday with his second wife,
Christine*

A Legacy of Learning and Positivity

Arthur's greatest passion was history, which he brought to life through tireless research, documentation, and the many books he authored. He was driven by a need to "never be stuck in a rut," constantly seeking new experiences, meeting new people, and expanding his knowledge. With a positive attitude and a great sense of humour, he was always ready to help others, leaving a lasting impact on his family and community. His children, Susan, Angela, Elizabeth, David, and Steven, remember him with love and gratitude.

David Clamp, 2025

A Legacy of Local History

Below is the story of how Arthur L Clamp began writing books, in his own words, drafted shortly before he passed away in 2001. I have only made minor alterations to this text, correcting grammatical errors that he did not survive to correct himself. When I first discovered this text, I was shocked to see my name mentioned. It seems that, unbeknownst to me, I shared my first PC with him. I suspect he used it during the day when I was at school, although I do have one memory of sitting with him and showing him how it worked. It has been a pleasure to pick up where he left off and see his books republished and redistributed, and to know that I was part of the story, even back then. It was also fascinating to discover that his pricing structure matches the way I have tried to price the books, with a third going to local sellers and the rest covering printing costs with a little left over for my expenses.

I am his eldest grandson, and it is a privilege to curate his legacy, which we are calling 'The Clamp Collection'. The very last line of the text originally reads "The following pages list all the titles." Sadly, that page is missing and we have no record of all the books he published and knowing that some of those were researched by other authors makes the process of finding them even harder. I look forward to one day completing the collection and seeing them all available again. And maybe, one day, I'll even start writing my own to add to the series. For now, here is his story in his own words.

Steven Gibson, 2025

Writing and Publishing Booklets on Local Topics and Areas

I started this interest in either 1968 or 1969 when living in Woodford. I had by these dates established the Department of Printing and I think I must have been looking for something different to do. The first titles were of A5 size proofed from type set at Clarke, Doble and Brendon, Ltd., Plymouth printers, and then made up into pages and printed at Sawtell and Neilson, Ltd., Totnes.

Then began a slow process of getting them out to shops, etc. which proved to be more time consuming and difficult than actually researching, writing and getting the books into print. However, I persisted and opened a business account with Barclays Bank on the Broadway. I was advised to give it a title so I called it "Westway Publications". There came along another problem, one of storage of paper and finished books which was solved when the family moved to Elburton in 1970.

I changed the printer to Penwell, Ltd., Callington, Cornwall, as he was then just setting up himself and his prices seemed very reasonable. I did not get any of the printers to make up the complete books. I hand folded the flat printed sheets, stitched the books on a small manual table stitcher and trimmed them in a small hand turned guillotine which I bought from someone in Penzance for £40. It was brought up in a van.

The trouble and time going to and fro to Callington was too much so I transferred the printing to PDS Printers, Prince Rock, Plymouth, and I have been with them ever since. Now they are at Plympton which is easy to reach and they fold the flat sheets which was turning out to be a long chore which only saved a small part of the printing costs.

All my first titles were written by myself. I took the photographs and developed them in the loft of the house, the type was set by now on a computer situated in the house at Elburton from which I had collected photographic lengths of text to cut up and law down as pages.

At some point I decided that I would do my own film processing of lith film so I bought a large second hand process camera from Kingsbridge and learnt through trial and error to make line negatives of the text and halftone negatives of the illustrations which proved more difficult than I anticipated. The main problem was trying to keep the developer in the large dish at the correct temperature as any change would affect the developing time. I replaced this old camera with a brand new one bought from Croydon, Surrey, costing £900. This has turned out to be a great asset cutting out an expensive part of the printer's costs and one crucial aspect of the work which I could control.

By the middle 1970s there were many outlets I had contacted in Plymouth, up to Dartmoor, Exeter, around to Torbay, Totnes, Dartmouth and the South Hams. The market for local books was much greater than I had first thought and through getting to know many local people undertaking research themselves had the chance to help and make up books for other people who had in most instances, got together a collection of photographs with some text in a rather muddled way. Through my experience in print I was able to shape up their work and get it into print and in every case I had to pay the printer and let the person have the royalties. In the majority of titles produced in this manner this was another way of producing titles and it did give some profit to my work. However, I must say that in a few cases I lost out by either the other person getting the numbers wrong, not returning any monies from stock I delivered or they thought that more of their books should have been sold.

The print run was usually 1,000 copies and from time to time I have had reprints of 250 copies. It took about ten years to clear the first print run so I always had large stocks in the garage, workshop, etc. The numbers sold during the early years was about 7,000 copies a year increasing to around 9,000 copies and for the whole of the enterprise about 500,000 have been sold. The booklets have become part of the local scene and many people collect them, shops regularly order copies and I go around certain areas month by month restocking or replacing titles as necessary.

During the past year or so I have started setting the text on a Packard Bell PC, something which I should have done some years back. I share it with Steven Gibson, my grandson. There appears to be no end to the market for local books, but I could not earn a regular income because of the long time it takes to sell stock.

However, now exceeding 100 titles made up mainly of A4 twenty-four page booklets, some folded guides, with selling prices set with a third going to the shop which is the trade custom, the original idea has been quite successful and could go on for ever.

Apart from monetary benefits, however spasmodically these might be, I have learnt a lot myself, met many interesting people and have become part of the local scene with requests to give talks and to advise people about getting into print.

Arthur L Clamp, 2001

Death of local historical author

'He was an incredible character who was just loved by everybody who knew him'

A WELL-loved Elburton author has died at the age of 68.

Arthur Clamp (pictured right), who was one of the West Country's most successful writers, died at St Luke's Hospice, Turnchapel, after losing his battle against cancer.

Tributes have been flooding in for a man who was known in the community as a prominent writer and outgoing person.

He produced more than 140 titles during his life, dealing with both fiction, fact and history, often discussing West Country topics that were close to his heart.

One of his most acclaimed books was *The Plymouth Blitz*, and he also won credit for *The Rise and Fall of the Bearings of Membland Hall*, set in Noss Mayo.

He achieved sales of between 7,000 and 9,000 books every year and it is estimated that he has sold over half a million books, covering the areas of Plymouth, Dartmoor, Exeter, Torbay and the South Hams.

Mr Clamp was born in Mitcham, Surrey, in 1932, and was the eldest of four children.

He moved to Devon in 1941 to avoid the London air-raids.

Mr Clamp trained as a printer in Exeter and also gained a teachers' certificate in 1959 from Garnet College in London.

Plymouth College of Art, however, was to prove to be Mr Clamp's working home for the following 32 years until 1991, when he retired as head of the printing department.

He had a great interest in travel and had visited the USA, Tanzania, China, Russia, Peru, as well as travelling across Europe, where he presented talks and slide shows on his experiences as a writer.

Mr Clamp was a member of Elburton Methodist Church for many years, superintendent of the Sunday school and editor of the church newsletter, as well as being involved in much charity work.

He was president of the Plymouth and District Field Club and an active member of the Elburton Residents' Association.

He enjoyed leading walks on Dartmoor and historical tours throughout the West Country.

Mr Clamp married his first wife, Rosemary, in 1956 and they had five children – Susan, Angela, Elizabeth, David and Steven – and she died in 1987. He also had 11 grandchildren.

He leaves a wife Christine, after remarrying in 1991, and her two children and three grandchildren.

'He was an incredible character who was just loved by everybody who knew him,' said his wife.

'He will be missed by his family, his friends, the people he worked with and just everybody who knew him through his books.'

More than 300 mourners attended his funeral at Elburton Methodist Church on Monday.

The attendance was a celebration of his life – he would have found that really special. It shows his vibrancy and love of people,' said Mrs Clamp.

Steven Clamp added that his father was 'a well respected and loved man, missed by a great many people throughout the South West and far beyond'.

This newspaper article, published by the Evening Herald on 17th August 2001, forms a good record of his life. Just as he encourages us to learn more about local history, we encourage you to learn a little about him. For that reason, we have included these pages at the back of all the most recently republished books, in honour of his memory and recognition of his contribution to the community.

www.ingramcontent.com/pod-product-compliance
Lightning Source LLC
Chambersburg PA
CBHW061404070526
44584CB00031B/4156